AF349122

# Interpretation of Scriptures

## Kingdom Knowledge and Understanding

Yvonne Smith

authorHOUSE®

*AuthorHouse*™
*1663 Liberty Drive*
*Bloomington, IN 47403*
*www.authorhouse.com*
*Phone: 1-800-839-8640*



*First published by AuthorHouse      12/27/2010*

*ISBN: 978-1-4520-7614-0 (sc)*
*ISBN: 978-1-4520-7615-7 (hc)*
*ISBN: 978-1-4520-7616-4 (e)*

*Library of Congress Control Number: 2010913948*

*Printed in the United States of America*

*This book is printed on acid-free paper.*

# Understanding the scriptures on a higher level

# (Genesis 2:28)

God says take control. Walk on it, through it, produce, set in motion to yield a return, then let it continue to reproduce after itself.

# (Genesis 12:2)

You shall be a blessing and help to others. Your name shall be prominent; you shall be gigantic nationwide; I will exalt thee.

# (Genesis 12:3)

God says, those who are the seed of Abraham, I will celebrate those that celebrate you. And I will denounce those that denounce you.

# (Genesis 26:12)

Isaac obeyed God and sowed in the place where God said to sow. He obtained an abundant harvest in the same year. The Lord's favor was all over him.

# (Exodus 15:6)

O Lord, thy right hand in power is glorious; the enemy is dashed to pieces, O Lord with thy right hand.

# (Leviticus 27:30)

It is holy unto the Lord, all the tithe of the Land.
(Your tithe money is HOLY unto the Lord)

The Lord adores thee and keeps thee.

# (Numbers 6:25)

The Lord makes his light shine upon you and be agreeable unto you.

# (Numbers 6:26)

The Lord's face be upon you, and peace be multiplied.

# (Numbers 6:27)

My name will be upon my chosen people. I will extol them.

# (Numbers 14:8)

If the Lord has joy in us, then he will bring us into this region, and give to us,a land that flows with abundance and favor.

# (Numbers 14:9)

Only obey the Lord, fear not the people of the land, for, they are edibles for usTheir protection is departed from them. The Lord is with us: fear not .

# (Numbers 20:8)

(Speak ye unto the rock: A commend method to bring forth what you want (God's way of doing things).

# (Numbers 20:11)

He smote the rock twice, taking the GLORY from God. Making it look like you're the one working the miracles. (Man's way of doing things.)

# (Deuteronomy 6:5)

With all thy power and strength, and with all thy mind, body, soul. And with all your heart, then cherish and love the Lord thy God.

# (Deuteronomy 7:6)

For they are a divinely blessed people unto God. The Lord thy God has selected you to be eccentric people in the world. Dedicated to him, ready to be used by him.

# (Deuteronomy 14:22)

Every business should tithe, for yearly increase.

# (Deuteronomy 14:23)

Whatever business,land, or product that you have obtained, the first check from it belongs to God, so that you will always revere God and know it was him that gave it to you. The blessing will come on it,so it will multiply!

# (Deuteronomy 14:24)

The place where God wants you to sow may not be in the country you live in.If not , send it by mail or Western Union.

# (Deuteronomy 14:25)

Pray and ask God where he wants you to plant your money seed. Remember, each ground has different breakthrough soil.

# (Deuteronomy 14:26)

You will take money and buy what you desire, no matter what it is. Lusting after whatever, not concerned about whether it pleases God or
(Not)
(State of mind without the Holy Ghost)
(Backsliding State of mind of the Believer)


I'll just do it this time and that's it. God's mercies are new everyday . He'll forgive me. He always does. Yes, with your lips, and not in your heart. We get so caught up in the moment of whatever were doing. We get so totally caught up we forget that *God is* <u>watching! He</u> sees where, what, when, and whom you have put above his statues and laws. Many have deceived themselves and now make excuses for why they do what they do. Just because a person has gotten by with something, that doesn't mean that they have gotten away with it. When Judgment Day comes, each person will have to stand alone and receive his or her judgment.

# (Deuteronomy 15:6)

Thou shall entrust to many nationalities, but thou shall not borrow.

# (Deuteronomy 23:4)

Because they hated you; they could not care less whether you had bread or water. They didn't want you come out of bondage so they went to the root worker, they went to, the witches, they cast spells, used black magic, mojos , charms, roots, stones, silver and gold dust, plastic, nails, staples , strings, straw, crafts, and food, just to name a few items, to curse thee.

# (Deuteronomy 28:22)

The Lord shall hit thee with swelling and with a fever, and with an infection, and with excessive burning, and with the sword, and with blasting, and mildew; they shall hunt thee until you die.

# (Deuteronomy 31:27)

For I know thy insurrection, and thy disobedience.

# (Ruth 2:12)

Because thou has learned to trust the Lord God of Israel, the Lord will recompense thy work and give you a full reward.

# (1 Samuel 3:20)

Samuel was ordained to be a prophet of the Lord. And Israel from Dan even to Beersheba recognized it.

# (1 Kings 6:38)

Bul = October/November

Eight = New beginnings

# (2 Kings 2:14)

He is always present and waiting to show himself
strong on the behalf of his people.

## (2 Kings 6:16)

He answered. Don't be apprehensive: for there are more of us, than there are of them.

# (1 Chronicles 5:19)

Because they put their confidence in him, they cried to God in the war, and he was intreated of them.

# (1 Chronicles 16:22)

Saying, touch not my anointed prophets, and do them no harm!

# (2 Chronicles 20:15)

Don't be frightened or dismayed because of this large crowd, for the fight is not yours, but God's.

# (Ezra 3:7)

According to the grant that they had received from Cyrus King of Persia, they gave money also to the bricklayers and construction workers. They gave food, drink, and oil to the people of Zidon, and Tyre. And they brought cedar trees from Lebanon to the sea of Joppa.

# (Nehemiah 13:2)

God turned the denouncement into a windfall.

# (Job 5:19)

He shall deliver thee in six problems: indeed, no bad shall touch thee in seven.

# (Job 6:25)

Right words are potent!

# (Job 29:1)

Also Job prolonged his myth.

# (Job 29:2)

Oh God preserve me, "as you did in the past."

# (Job 29:3)

My head shined from the light of his candle, when I walked through darkness.

~ 41 ~

# (Job 29:4)

As in the days of my youth, when the hidden secret of God was upon my temple.

# (Job 29:5)

When God Almighty was also with me, when my children were about me.

# (Job 29:6)

When I cleaned my steps with butter, rivers of oil poured out from the rocks.

## (Job 29:7)

When I went out through the fence to the city,
when I prepared my seat in the road!

∾ 45 ∾

# (Job 29:8)

The young men hid themselves when they saw me; the elderly arose and stood up.

# (Job 29:9)

The princes stopped their dialogue and covered their mouths with their hands.

# (Job 29:10)

The dignified held their peace, and their vernacular cleaved to the roof of their mouth.

# (Job 29:11)

It blessed me when my ears heard it gave witness to me when my eyes saw.

# (Job 29:12)

Because I liberated the poor that wept and the orphans and the people that had no help.

# (Job 29:13)

The approbation of him that was ready to die had approached me and caused the widow's heart to sing for joy.

# (Job 29:14)

I put on truth, and it dressed me: my decisions were as a cape and a diadem.

# (Job 29:15)

To the blind, I was eyes, and to the lame I was feet.

# (Job 29:16)

I was a father to the impoverished: and I knew not the cause I was searching for.

# (Job 29:17)

And I will stop the mouths of the ungodly and yank the spoil out of his teeth.

# (Job 29:18)

Then Job said, shall I die in my nest? And shall
I multiply my days as the sand?

# (Job 29:19)

My root was dispersed by the waters, and the moisture of the morning lay all night upon my limb.

# (Job 29:20)

My glory was refreshed, and my bow restored in my hands.

# (Job 29:21)

Men listened to me, and my counsel and kept silent.

# (Job 29:22)

After I spoke , they spoke no more, and my speech collapsed upon them.

## (Job 29:23)

And they watched me as if looking for the rain,
and they spreading their mouths wide.

# (Job 29:24)

If I laughed, they in matter believed it, and they could not remove the shine from my face.

# (Job 37:23)

Touching the Almighty God, we cannot find him out. He is wonderful in dominion, and in wisdom, and in abundance of rectitude: he will not agitate.

# (Psalms 7:11)

God forms his opinion of the righteous. Every day God is furious with the wicked.

# (Psalms 8:6)

You have put all things under his feet. You have
made him to rule over the labor of his hands.

# (Psalms 11:3)

The righteous can run straight to Jesus, who is the solid (rock) foundation.

# (Psalms 25:1)

O Lord, unto thee do I raise up my soul.

# (Psalms 25:2)

O my God, let me not be embarrassed. Do not let my foes triumph over me, for I trust in thee.

# (Psalms 25:3)

Yea , let none be humiliated that wait on thee. Let them be mortified that offend without cause.

# (Psalms 25:4)

Reveal to me thy techniques, O Lord; instill in me thy routes.

# (Psalms 25:5)

All day I wait on thee. Steer me in thy truth and educate me, for thou are the God of my salvation.

# (Psalms 25:6)

Retain, O Lord, thy tender leniency and affectionate character, for they have been ever ancient.

# (Psalms 25:7)

O Lord, according to thy clemancy, remember thou me for thy righteous sake. Recall not the transgressions of my youth or my sins.

# (Psalms 25:8)

Genuine and erect is the Lord: therefore, he will teach sinners the way.

# (Psalms 25:9)

The domestic will he guide in judgement, and the domesticated will he teach his way.

# (Psalms 25:10)

All the paths of the Lord are forgiveness and honesty for those who keep his agreement and his testimonies.

# (Psalms 25:11)

O Lord, for thy name's sake, pardon my sins, for they are great.

# (Psalms 25:12)

The man that fears the Lord, he shall teach him in the way that he chooses.

# (Psalms 25:13)

His soul shall inhabit comfort, and his seed shall possess the earth.

# (Psalms 25:14)

The Lord shall reveal hidden secrets to those who revere him.

# (Psalms 25:15)

My eyes are continuously toward the Lord, for he will snatch my feet out of the net.

# (Psalms 25:16)

Turn unto me, and have consideration upon me, for I am desolate and troubled.

# (Psalms 25:17)

The distresses of my heart are wide: O bring me out of my misery.

# (Psalms 25:18)

Consider my grief and pain and forgive all my iniquities.

# (Psalms 25:19)

My enemies are many. They hate with ferocious hatred.

# (Psalms 25:20)

O how my soul trusts in thee. Keep and deliver me, for I will not be ashamed.

# (Psalms 25:21)

On thee do I wait. Let worthiness and erectness preserve me.

# (Psalms 25:22)

Retrieve Israel, O God, out of all its distresses.

# (Psalms 25:23)

Hear my voice of supplication when I weep, and when I lift my hands-up toward your consecrated authority.

# (Psalms 29:4)

The Lord's voice is robust. The Lord's voice is full of grandeur.

# (Psalms 33:1)

Delight in the Lord, O ye righteous, for praise is what the upright do.

# (Psalms 33:2)

Praise the Lord harmoniously. Sing to him. Play an instrument of ten strings.

# (Psalms 33:3)

Sing to him a new melody. Play ingeniously with a loud sound.

# (Psalms 33:4)

For the word of the Lord is correct, and all his works are complete and accurate.

# (Psalms 33:5)

Righteousness he loves, and judgment. The Lord is full of goodness in the earth.

# (Psalms 33:6)

By the breath of his mouth. By the word of the Lord all the host of the heavens were made.

# (Psalms 33:7)

The waters of the sea he gathers together as a heap. In depth he lays up storehouses.

# (Psalms 33:8)

Let all the earth revere the Lord: let all the people of the world stand in astonishment of him.

# (Psalms 33:9)

For he spoke, and it was complete. He ordered, and it stood firm.

# (Psalms 33:10)

The Lord takes the opinion of the heathen to be of none effect obsolete: he makes the devices of the people irrelevant.

# (Psalms 33:11)

The guidance of the Lord abides forever, the sentiments of his heart to all generations.

# (Psalms 33:12)

Blessed is the kingdom whose Jehovah God is the Lord, and the people he has chosen as his own heir.

# (Psalms 33:13)

The Lord views from heaven; he observes all the sons of men.

# (Psalms 33:14)

From the place of his holy lodging he looks upon all of earth's inhabitants.

# (Psalms 33:15)

He creates their hearts similar; he ponders all their works.

# (Psalms 33:16)

There is no king preserved by the crowd: a powerful man is not delivered by substantial strength.

# (Psalms 33:17)

A car is a vain thing to put trust in: neither shall he rescue any by his enormous power.

# (Psalms 33:18)

Look, the Lord's eye is upon those who reverence him, as well as those who trust in his mercy.

# (Psalms 33:19)

To rescue their soul from death, and to keep them alive in deficiency.

# (Psalms 33:20)

Our soul tarries for the Lord: he is our support
and our protection.

# (Psalms 33:21)

For our heart shall delight in him, because in his holy name we are loyal.

# (Psalms 33:22)

Let thy compassion, O Lord, be upon us, consequently, as we trust in thee.

# (Psalms 35:27)

Let those who patronize my righteous cause yell for joy, and be gratified. Let them say consecutively, let the Lord be magnified, which both delight in the prosperity of his servant.

⌘ 113 ⌘

# (Psalms 62:11)

God has pronounced once; twice have I heard this: that predominance belongeth unto God.

# (Psalms 83:5)

For they have deliberated together all in agreement: they are abettors against thee.

# (Psalms 104:15)

And the blood of Jesus that makes the heart of man glad. And the Holy Ghost that makes his face shine, and the Word of God that strengthens man's heart.

# (Psalms 107:23)

They do illustrious business in the waters: the cruise that goes down through the sea.

# (Psalms 117:1)

O glorify the Lord, all ye nations: extol him all ye people.

# (Psalms 117:2)

Praise the Lord. The authenticity of the Lord continues forever. For his sympathetic kindness is momentous toward us.

# (Psalms 120:1)

The Lord heard me, in all my distress when I
cried out to him.

# (Psalms 120:2)

Rescue my soul, O Lord, from false lips, and from a deceptive tongue.

# (Psalms 120:3)

What shall be presented unto thee? Or what shall be done unto thee, thou deceitful tongue?

(Psalms 120:4)

The fortified with sharp arrows and juniper of coals.

# (Psalms 120:5)

It makes me grieve that I dwell in Mesech, and that I dwell in the tent of Kedar!

# (Psalms 120:6)

My body has abided long with him that despiseth tranquillity.

# (Psalms 120:7)

I am for tranquillity: but when I talk, they are for contentions.

# (Psalms 139:14)

I will worship and honor thee; for I am skillfully astoundingly, marvelously, amazingly created.

# (Psalms 140:3)

Place a patrol, O Lord, before my mouth. Maintain the gate of my lips.

# (Proverbs 8:12)

I knowledge inhabits with vigilance, and find out comprehensive information of witty inventions.

# (Proverbs 18:22)

God reveals to the man who his wife is he tells him if don't know her location. When God gives a man a wife it is for the unifying of the two a completion, that God ordained. Each one has what the other needs in some area, strength to hold the other up when needed. It's a good thing,because all qualities complement each other . A true marriage made in heaven! In order to obtain the Lord's favor, you must appreciate that God loves you enough to prepare you and give you one who you need that humanly satisfies your physical needs.

(Proverbs 31:22)

She designs her veils and embroides them herself. Her clothes are made of silk and purple threads.

# (Proverbs 31:24)

She designs fabrics and markets them. And she sells undergarments to the retailer.

# (Ecclesiastes 4:9)

For their labor they have a good reward, because two are better than one.

# (Ecclesiastes 5:3)

For vision comes through a variety of opportunities.

# (Ecclesiastes 7:8)

Better is the completion of a thing than the start of it; and the patient in spirit is better than the conceited in spirit.

# (Ecclesiastes 7:12)

For erudition is a protection, and money is a defense, but the superiority of knowledge is. that wisdom gives life to them that have it.

# (Ecclesiastes 7:19)

Intelligence substantiates the informed more than ten mighty men in the city.

# (Isaiah 30:20)

The Lord will allow adversity and affliction. Sometimes he will allow the very person that taught you to afflict you. Your own teacher! That's why you must know God for yourself and be obedient to God and learn his Holy word so no matter what, you can overcome.

# (Isaiah 30:21)

Your ears will hear the word of the Holy Ghost.
This is the way; walk in it. Words of direction.
This is God's way or God is not in this.

# (Isaiah 30:23)

Then shall he rain on your seed, that you shall sow the ground with it, and the substance of increase from the ground shall be pomp and profuse. Your stock shall feed on large grazing grounds in that day.

# (Isaiah 40:5)

And the glory of the Lord shall be disclosed and all creation shall view it together; for out of the Lord's mouth it has been spoken.

# (Isaiah 45:3)

I will give you the wealth of the world, and the unseen hidden places of money,that you may know that I, the Lord, called you by name. I am the God of Israel.

# (Isaiah 46:10)

Professing the completion from the start, and from old times the things that are not complete, my advice will stand, and I will do all my pleasure.

# (Isaiah 51:2)

Examine Abraham, your father, and Sarah that bore you, for I alone called him, and enlarged him and favored him.

# (Isaiah 59:21)

This is my agreement with them, the Lord said. My courage that is upon you and my words that I have put in your mouth shall not leaveyour mouth, nor the mouths of your children, nor the mouths of your children's children, the Lord said, from now and forever.

# (Isaiah 65:5)

They say, I am holier than you are endure
alone.

# (Isaiah 65:24)

And it shall be that before they ask, I will reply.
And while they are yet talking, I will respond.

# (Jeremiah 1:8)

The Lord said, I am with you and I will deliver you. Don't be afraid of their faces.

# (Jeremiah 10:10)

The nations shall not be able to abide his wrath. At his indignation the earth shall tremble. But the Lord is an everlasting king, the true God. He is the living God.

# (Jeremiah 22:13)

The person who builds his house by unrighteousness and uses his neighbor's service without paying him for his work will be in trouble.

# (Jeremiah 51:20)

I will demolish kingdoms. I will smash in places the nations for thee. Thou are my battle axe and weapons of war.

# (Lamentations 3:15)

They clap their hands as you pass by them. They make disapproving sounds.The perfection of beauty called by man is this the city? The joy of the whole earth?

# (Ezekiel 7:25)

Devastation cometh; they shall seek peace, and there shall be none.

# (Ezekiel 7:26)

The law shall depart from the preacher andfrom the ancients' counsel.Evil shall follow evil, and gossip shall follow gossip. Then shall they seek revelation from the prophet.

# (Ezekiel 7:27)

They shall know that I am the Lord. I will judge them according to the way they judge. I will do unto them as they do to others. The people of land hands shall be troubled. The king shall suffer, and the prince shall be clothed with desolation.

# (Ezekiel 8:7)

Behold, the holes that are in your walls, are to be known as great abominations that are done by the wicked.

# (Ezekiel 20:27)

Son of man, speak unto the church say unto them, thus saith the Lord God. Besides, in this your fathers have spoken evil of me. In doing so they have committed a trespass against me.

# (Ezekiel 20:39)

O church, thus saith the Lord God. Go serve everyone his idols from now on if you will not listen to me, but do not contaminate my holy name with your gifts or idols.

# (Ezekiel 22:18)

Son of man, the church has become to me worthless. They are all brass and tin, iron and lead. In the mist of the fire, they are even the dross of silver.

# (Ezekiel 22:30)

Say unto the church, thus saith the Lord God.
Are you contaminated following the manner
of your fathers? And perpetrate whoredoms
subsequently like their abominations.

# (Ezekiel 34:26)

There shall be downpours of favor. I will make them and the places around my hill a blessing. I will cause the rain to come down in his season.

# (Ezekiel 44:30)

So that he may cause the blessing to rest in thine house, give unto the priest the first of your money, and the first of all the highest increase of all things, and every sort of all your offerings.

# (St Matthew 6:24)

You cannot serve God and money. No man can serve two leaders: for he will either hate one or love the other or hold to one and despise the other.

# (St Matthew 12:13)

The man's hand was restored whole, like the other, when he stretched it forth.

# (St Matthew 12:15)

Jesus knew their plans and he departed from them. And he healed the great multitudes that followed him.

## (St Matthew 15:10)

So they could incriminate him, they asked him is it lawful to heal on the Sabbath? Because there was a man whose hand was withered.

# (St Matthew 15:26)

He answered and said, I'm not obligated to take
the children's bread and give it to you.

# (St Matthew 21:31)

Which of the two did the Father's will? Jesus answered the first. Verily I say unto you, that the common people and the harlots will learn God's way of doing things before you.

# (St Matthew 21:32)

For John came unto you in the way of righteousness. You didn't believe. You saw it and didn't repent, but the harlots and publicans believed him.

# (St Matthew 25:4)

But the intelligent took oil in their containers
with their lamps.

❧ 170 ❧

# (St Mark 4:28)

The earth introduces increase of her own kind; waiting/ 1) Blade time 2) Stalk time 3) Harvest time.

# (St Mark 7:18)

Understand, what comes out of the mouth comes
from what's in a man's heart.

# (St Mark 7:19)

For out of the heart comes evil and wicked thoughts, which defile a man.

# (St Mark 9:23)

Jesus said to him, if you have the ability to believe, all things are achievable.

# (St Mark 10:25)

It is simpler for a camel to go through the eye of a needle than for a wealthy man to enter into God's way of doing things.

# (St Mark 10:30)

But he shall receive a hundred fold in this lifetime, buildings, and brethren, sisters, mothers, children and estates, fields, islands, shores, farms, countries, with harassment ill treatment; and in the world to come eternal life.

# (St Luke 4:30)

But he proceeded through the center of them
and went on his way.

# (St Luke 6:38)

Give, and it shall be given unto you; good volume, compressed down, shaken jointly, and over flowing, shall men give into your bosom. For the same volume you allocate it shall be measured to you again.

# (St Luke 12:6)

Five sparrows are sold for two farthings. And
God has not forgotten one.

# (St Luke 16:15)

It came to pass, when he returned, the kingdom being received, then he bade the servants to come to him, whom he had given the capital, so he might find out how much every man had acquired by trafficking.

# (St Luke 19:23)

Why haven't you put my money into the treasury, so that when I arrived I could claim it with interest?

# (St Luke 24:31)

Their eyes were uncovered. They knew him, and he disappeared out of their view.

# (St Luke 24:36)

As they were speaking, Jesus stood in the center of them and said, Shalom be unto you.

# (St John 3:8)

The wind moves where it whistles. You hear the sound but can't tell when it comes or when it goes: so are the people that are born of the spirit.

# (St John 4:14)

But anyone who drinks the water I give him shall never thirst or crave again:the water that I shall give him shall be in him, a well of living water springing up into everlasting life.

# (St John 4:38)

I sent you to harvest where you put no labor:
other men worked, and you are entered into
their parturition.

# (St John 6:27)

Work not for meat that will perish, but for meat that will last forever. Which the son of man shall give unto you: for him God the Father have sealed.

# (St John 6:44)

Except the father draw him to me whom he sent, no man can come and I will raise him up at the last day.

# (St John 6:51)

I am the living substance that came down from heaven. If any man eats this bread, he shall live forever. The bread that I will give is my body, which I give for the life of the world.

# (St John 6:63)

They are spirit, and they are life, the words that I speak unto you it is the spirit that accelerates; the flesh gains nothing.

# (St John 8:12)

Then Jesus spake again, saying, he who follows me shall not walk in darkness but shall have the light of life, for I am the light of the world.

# (St John 8:23)

He said unto them, I am not of this world. I am
from above. You are of this world.

# (St John 8:31)

Jesus said to the Jews who believed in him, you are indeed my disciples, if you proceed in my word.

# (St John 8:32)

And you shall know the truth and the truth shall free you .

# (St John 8:47)

He that belongs to God hears God's words. He that doesn't hear is not of God.

# (St John 9:3)

Jesus answered, neither this man nor his parents have sinned, but that God works should be made evident in him.

# (St John 10:3)

The watchman openth; and leads them out his
voice the sheep hears: by name he calleth his
sheep.

# (St. John 10:10)

The burglar comes only to rob, kill, and demolish: I am (Jesus) came that they might live, and have it more abundantly.

# (St. John 10:27)

They follow me. I know who they are. My sheep hear my voice.

# (St. John 10:28)

No man shall snatch them out of my hand. They shall not perish, and I will give them eternal life.

# (St. John 11:4)

Jesus heard that and said, for the glory of God and that the son of God might be glorified in it. This sickness is not unto death.

# (St. John 14:21)

He who loves me will I manifest myself to him, he that has my commandments, and keep them, and he that loves me shall be loved of my father.

# (St. John 15:16)

You have not selected me but I have selected you, and appointed you that you should go and bring forth fruit, and that your fruit should endure, so that anything you ask my father in my name, he may give to you.

# (St. John 16:14)

He shall worship me: and receive the ones that belong unto me, and show it to you.

# (St. John 16:23)

Truly, truly, I say unto you, in that day you shall ask me nothing. Anything you ask the father in my name, he will give to you.

# (Acts 2:38)

Peter said to them, for the remission of sins, repent and be baptized, everyone,in the name of Jesus Christ, and the gift of the Holy Ghost you shall receive.

(Acts 4:29)

Now Lord, observe their threats and grant thy
servants boldness so they may speak thy word.

# (Acts 4:30)

By spreading your hand out, signs and wonder may be done to heal in the name of the holy child Jesus.

(Acts 4:37)

The money from the land sold, bring it and lay it at the apostles' feet.

## (Acts 5:9)

Peter said to her, how is it that you have harmonized together to lie to the spirit of the Lord? Observe, the feet of them which buried thy husband shall carry you out the door.

# (Acts 5:19)

The angel of the Lord brought them forth and opened the prison doors.

(Acts 5:23)

The keepers were standing outside. We found the prison indeed secure, but we found no man inside when we opened the doors.

(Acts 5:32)

God has given to those who obey the Holy Ghost.

# (Acts 6:3)

Brethren, designate over this business seven trustworthy men from among you, full of the Holy Ghost and wisdom.

(Acts 6:7)

The word of God intensifies; in Jerusalem, the disciples' number multiplied greatly; obedient to the faith were a large group of priests.

# (Acts 8:39)

When they came out of the water, Phillip was taken away by the spirit of the Lord, he saw him no more the Eunuch went his way rejoicing.

# (Acts 10:40)

Openly God showed him Jesus that was raised up on the third day.

∽ 217 ∽

## (Acts 10:41)

He rose from the dead and did eat and drink with them. Not with all, but with preferred witnesses God had chosen.

# (Acts 12:9)

He thought it was a dream, what the angel had done, but it was true. He went out and followed him.

# (Acts 12:17)

Peter commanded them with his hand to hold their peace, telling them how the Lord delivered him out of prison. Go show James and the brethren, he said. Then he went to another place.

# (Acts 13:47)

Look, you haters, and wonder and perish: in your days, I work a work that you shall not accept, though a man affirm it unto you.

# (Acts 14:22)

We must enter into the kingdom of God through much tribulation, validating the souls of the disciples, advising them to continue in the faith.

(Acts 14:27)

The church gathered together. They repeated
all that God had done with them and how he
expanded the door of faith to the Gentiles.

# (Acts 17:15)

Receiving a command, Silas and Timothas departed with total quickness and came unto Paul.

## (Acts 20:10)

Paul said, don't trouble yourselves. He is still alive. He fell on him and hugged him.

# (Acts 22:13)

He came, stood, and said to me, Brother Saul, obtain your eyesight. And the same hour I glanced upon him.

# (Acts 22:14)

Hear the words of his mouth, the God of our father has selected you, that you should know his desire and see that just one Jesus.

# (Acts 2616)

Rise and stand upon your feet: for this intention have I appeared unto you to make you a minister and testimony of the things you have seen, and those things I will emanate unto you.

(Acts 26: 23)

That Christ should suffer, and show light unto the Gentiles and the people, that he should be the first to rise from the dead.

# (Acts 28:8)

Paul entered and prayed for Publius's father. He laid hand on him and he was healed of a fever and a blood issue.

# (Acts 28:9)

Others on the island who had diseases were healed.

# (Acts 28:31)

With all assurance, preach the kingdom of God. Teach those things concerning the Lord Jesus Christ. Let no man prohibit you.

# (Romans 1:18)

For the anger in God is exposed from heaven against all unholiness and unrighteousness of man, who hold the veracity in unrighteousness.

# (Romans 1:19)

Because that which may be comprehended of God is evident in them; for God hath revealed it unto them.

# (Romans 1:20)

For the imperceptible things of him from the creature of the world are clearly discern, being understood by the things that are made, even his infinite predominance and God head, so that they are without explanation.

# (Romans 1:21)

Because when they knew God, they revered him not as God neither were grateful; but became conceited in there ideas, and their idiotic heart was darkened.

# (Romans 1:22)

Professing to be superior, they became idiots.

# (Romans 1:23)

And changed the eminence of the scrupulous God into reflection made like a demoralized man, to birds. Four-footed beasts and creeping things.

# (Romans 1:24)

God gave them up to filthiness through the craving of their own hearts, to disgrace their own bodies among themselves.

# (Romans 1:25)

Who altered the authenticity of God into a lie and idolized and served the creature more than the creator, who is blessed forever. Amen.

# (Romans 1:26)

For this effect, God gave them up unto sinful feelings. Even the women changed the original use into that which is in disagreement with nature.

# (Romans 1:27)

Also likewise the men, leaving the original use of the woman, burned with desire, one toward another men with men active in that which is unnatural, receiving recompense of their fault which was fulfill.

# (Romans 1:28)

They did not prefer to keep God in their cognizance. A reprobate mind God gave them, to do things that were not appropriate.

# (Romans 1:29)

With existence of sex outside of marriage, unethical, blasphemous, intentions to hurt others, greedy; full of jealousy, slander, despute, guile, revile, keeping no secrets.

# (Romans 1:30)

God hates, gossip, slander. The arrogant, braggers, creators of evil things..

# (Romans 1:31)

Not comprehending, breakers of agreement not in possession of natural feelings, having no mercy.

# (Romans 1:32)

They who know God's judgment, which perpetrate such things deserving death, delight in those who do likewise.

# (Romans 4:17)

It is written, God, whom he believed, who expedite the lifeless and calls things as they were, have made you a father of many nations.

# (Romans 8:24)

For we are saved by faith: but expectation seen is not optimism: for what a man look at, why have yet anticipation for it.

# (Romans 8:25)

But we wait patiently with expectancy for that which is not seen.

# (Romans 16:25)

Now the secret revelation mystery, which was kept since the world began, is the power of him, Jesus Christ, to establish you according to the gospel preached.

# (1 Corinthians 4:20)

For the word is power in the kingdom of God.

# (2 Corinthians 4:18)

Although we view not the things that are visible but things that are invisible: things that are visible are secular, but things that are invisible are everlasting, unchangeable.

# (2 Corinthians 7:1)

Dearly beloved, revere God. Let us purify ourselves from all pollution of the flesh and spirit, flawless and sacred, in order to possess these promises.

# (2 Corinthians 7:1)

Thank God for his gift, which exists but which is not talked about.

# (Galatians 3:8)

Through Abraham's faith, all nations shall be blessed. The scriptures know that God would justify the heathen through the gospel being preached.

## ( Ephesians 6: 10)

Finally, in the authority of his strength, brethren, be sturdy in the Lord.

# (Colossians 2:10)

God is head authority over all invisible spirits.
For they were created by him and for him.

# (1 Thessalonians 4:11)

We order you, be quiet and study. Work to own
your own business.

# (2 Thessalonians 3:11)

Some walk among you for chaoes, which are gossipers, not working at all.

# (1 Timothy 1:5)

Love is commanded out of a clean heart, now having the ability to recognize faith that is false.

# (Hebrews 1:3)

The majesty whose existence is brilliant proceeding his glory. The express representation of his personality. Justifying all things by the power of his word. He sits at the right hand of God on high.

❧ 262 ☙

# (Hebrews 6:12)

In no manner be lazy. Support them who through trust and endurance receive the promises.

# (Hebrews 10:36)

Ye have need of endurance, that ye may obtain the promise, after the will of God is complete.

# (James 5:4)

Behold the Lord of host's ears are open to the cares of the employed, which wages is kept back by deception, the money crieth.

# (James 5:13)

Is any joyful? Sing melodies. Is any troubled?
Pray.

# (1 John 3:22)

In his sight we do things that are agreeable, because we keep his rules. Anything we request, we obtain of him.

# (2 John 1:10)

If any come and not introduce this teaching, God
swiftness show not unto him. Neither receive
him into your house.

# (Revelation 2:9)

I know the affliction and lack of them which are chosen. ( But I say thou art rich). The church of Satan's works are irreverent.

# (Revelation 21:6)

Freely I give unto him that desire to drink of life's water spring. It is complete. I am Alpha, the beginning, and Omega the end.

# About the Author

I am a woman filled with the Holy Spirit who lives a consecrated life and obedient to God, by which he has given me revelation knowledge of the Scriptures. These are courses I have completed: Light University/Certificate of Completion 2007 biblical counseling course. Certificate of Completion marriage mentoring course 2008. Grace Bible College and Seminary/Associate Degree in Bible Studies 2008. Certificate of Completion Halley Bible Commentary 2008.

www.ingramcontent.com/pod-product-compliance
Lightning Source LLC
LaVergne TN
LVHW091556200325
806443LV00003B/112/J